1944

MOLLY'S
COOK
BOOK

*A Peek at
Dining in the
Past with Meals
You Can Cook Today*

PLEASANT COMPANY PUBLICATIONS, INC.

First Edition.
Printed in the United States of America.
95 96 97 98 99 WCR 10 9 8 7 6 5 4 3

PICTURE CREDITS
The following individuals and organizations have generously
given permission to reprint illustrations in this book:
Page 1—Library of Congress; 2—National Archives; 6—Kellogg Company;
7—The Archives of Labor and Urban Affairs, Wayne State University;
9—FDR Museum; 13—© The Cudahy Packing Co., 1948; 15—The CHIQUITA®
logo is a registered trademark of Chiquita Brands, Inc. (top); 20th Century Fox Film
Corporation (bottom); 17— Library of Congress; 19—JELL-O® is a registered
trademark of Kraft General Foods, Inc. Used with permission.; 20—Wisconsin Center
for Film and Theater Research; 23—Geo. A. Hormel & Co.; 25—Grand Met Pillsbury
Co.; 26—Camera Guild Inc., NY; 29—State Historical Society of Wisconsin;
30 —Walter Sanders, LIFE Magazine © Time Warner Inc., Set #11980;
33—Cannon Percale Sheets—reproduced with permission of Fieldcrest Cannon, Inc.;
34—Reproduced with the permission of General Mills, Inc.; 35, 37—Westinghouse
Electric Corporation; 39—Taken from *Kitchen Culture, Fifty Years of Food Fads*, by
Gerry Schremp, © 1991 (bottom); 41—State Historical Society of Wisconsin;
42 —Gordon Coster, LIFE Magazine © Time Warner Inc., Set #12084;
43—Nina Leen, LIFE Magazine © Time Warner Inc., Set #16441;
44—Gordon Coster, LIFE Magazine © Time Warner Inc., Set #12084.

Edited by Jodi Evert and Jeanne Thieme
Written by Polly Athan, Rebecca Sample Bernstein,
Terri Braun, Jodi Evert, and Jeanne Thieme
Designed and Art Directed by Jane S. Varda
Produced by Karen Bennett, Laura Paulini, and Pat Tuchscherer
Cover Illustration by Nick Backes
Inside Illustrations by Susan Mahal
Photography by Mark Salisbury
Historical and Picture Research by Polly Athan,
Rebecca Sample Bernstein, Terri Braun, Jodi Evert,
Robyn Hansen, and Doreen Smith
Recipe Testing Coordinated by Jean doPico
Food Styling by Janice Bell
Prop Research by Leslie Cakora

Library of Congress Cataloging-in-Publication Data

Molly's cookbook : a peek at dining in the past with meals you can cook today /
[edited by Jodi Evert and Jeanne Thieme ; written by Polly Athan . . . et al. ;
inside illustration by Susan Mahal]. — 1st ed.
p. cm.
ISBN 1-56247-117-1 (pbk.)
1. Cookery—Juvenile literature. 2. Cookery, American—Juvenile literature.
3. World War, 1939-1945—United States—Juvenile literature. 4. United States—Social
life and customs—1918-1945—Juvenile literature. I. Athan, Polly. II. McIntire, Molly.
III. Mahal, Susan.
TX652.5.M65 1994 641.5′123—dc20 94-17564 CIP AC

CONTENTS

S pecial thanks to all the children and adults who tested the recipes and gave us their valuable comments:

Maretta Babler and her mother Margot Babler
Laurie Barman and her mother Mary Barman
Megan Bielich and her mother Jane Bielich
Elizabeth Dorman and her mother Terry Dorman
Amanda Ganser and her mother Tam Ganser
Heidi Ganser and her mother Marie Ganser
Emily Heenan and her mother Doris Heenan
Rowan Hendrick and her mother Joanne Riese
Kirsten Hendrickson and her mother Patti Hendrickson
Ashley Holekamp and her mother Lynda Holekamp
Christine Klein and her mother Beverly Klein
Amanda Maffei and her mother Sharon Maffei
Melissa Martin and her mother Jeanette Martin
Meredith Nelson and her mother Ann Nelson
Meredith Newlin and her mother Karen Watson-Newlin
Elisabeth and Maureen O'Donnell and their mother Kathryn O'Donnell
Rebecca Russell and her mother Kathleen Russell
Tara Salbego and her mother Monica Schober
Katie Scallon and her mother Betsy Scallon
Paula Simons and her mother Janis Simons
Sienna Teschendorf and her mother Mary Anne Derheimer
Kristi Wendtland and her mother Jeanne Wendtland
Brooke Woestman and her mother Kris Woestman
Emily Ziegler and her mother Susan Ziegler

COOKING IN THE 1940S

During World War Two, when Molly was growing up, many American women had jobs outside their homes for the first time because so many men had left to fight in the war. Women no longer had as much time for cooking and housework, so their children had to help out. Most children on the home front did part of the cooking and cleanup for meals.

In 1944, Americans on the home front were more concerned with winning World War Two than

with cooking elegant meals. They were proud to be practical in the kitchen. When Molly, Mom, or Mrs. Gilford cooked, they knew that food was a valuable resource, and they didn't waste it. They found ways to use less meat, sugar, and butter, which were sometimes hard to get during the war.

MOLLY ★ 1944

Molly McIntire grew up on America's home front during World War Two. She helped prepare her family's meals with less meat and sugar and fewer canned vegetables so there would be more of those foods to send to soldiers.

Some things have changed since Molly was growing up. Today's kitchens are equipped with electric dishwashers and microwave ovens. Supermarkets sell frozen foods that are ready to heat and serve. And women and girls aren't the only ones who work in the kitchen. Men and boys cook, too.

Learning about kitchens and cooking in the past will help you understand what it was like to grow up the way Molly did. Cooking the meals she ate will bring history alive for you and your family today.

SHOPPING AND SHORTAGES

Some foods were hard to get on the home front during World War Two. Much of America's sugar, coffee, meat, cheese, and butter was shipped to faraway places where United States troops were fighting or where America's allies needed food.

Canned food was easier to ship across an ocean than fresh food. Fresh food spoiled and got squashed. Cans were easy to store. In places where there were no refrigerators, canned food didn't spoil. And canned food was easy to use. Soldier cooks simply had to heat and serve it. But metal for cans was scarce during World War Two. Factories were using all the steel and tin they could get for ships, tanks, guns, and bullets. In a short time, canned food became scarce on the home front.

To give every family on the home front a fair chance to get foods that were in short supply, the government started a system called *rationing*. Every man, woman, and child got a ration book full of red and blue stamps each month. The stamps were marked with numbers that told how many points the stamps were worth. People had to use points and money to buy things that were rationed.

For example, in 1944 a pound of butter cost 46 cents and 16 ration points. Customers had to give a store clerk both money and ration stamps to buy the butter. Without ration stamps, customers couldn't buy the butter. When they used up their ration stamps for butter, they had to wait until they got a new supply of ration stamps before they could buy more butter.

RATION STAMPS

Letters on ration stamps told when the stamps could be used. Numbers told how many points they were worth. Red points were for meat, cheese, sugar, butter, and oil. Blue points were for canned food. Tokens were used to make change for ration stamps. This grocer is trying to find out how many points his canned goods are worth.

SETTING MOLLY'S TABLE

Molly set her kitchen table with inexpensive dishes called Fiesta®, which were inspired by the colorful festivals of Mexico. Molly loved mixing and matching the beautiful rainbow shades. Ads for Fiesta said that the dishes had "great eye appeal that transforms eating from a humdrum routine to the zest of a party."

Molly set five places for dinner at the kitchen table. She and Jill got blue plates, and Brad and Mrs. Gilford got yellow plates. She saved a green plate, her least favorite color, for Ricky. Before the war, Molly and her family never ate dinner at the kitchen table. The whole family had dinner together in the dining room. Everyone shared the day's events and laughed at Dad's jokes and funny stories.

After Dad went away to take care of wounded soldiers, Mom often had to work late at the Red Cross headquarters. So Mrs. Gilford usually cooked dinner for Molly, her brothers, and her sister. When Mrs. Gilford served mashed turnips from the Victory garden, Molly just couldn't eat them. It didn't help that Ricky called them "old, cold, moldy brains." But when Mom came home and warmed the turnips with butter and sugar, Molly ate every forkful!

SONGS FOR KP

After meals, it was time for KP duty. KP stood for Kitchen Patrol, which was an army phrase for cooking and cleanup. Singing along with the family or the radio made KP more fun. See if anyone in your family can teach you to sing these hit songs from 1944:
"Sentimental Journey"
"Swinging on a Star"
"Don't Fence Me In"

From the book *Meet Molly*

TIPS FOR TODAY'S COOKS

MEASURING FLOUR

A good cook measures exactly. Here is a hint for measuring flour. Spoon the flour into a measuring cup, heaping it up over the top. Then use the spoon handle to level off the flour. Don't shake or tap the cup.

TABLE OF MEASUREMENTS

3 teaspoons = 1 tablespoon
2 cups = 1 pint
2 pints = 1 quart
4 cups = 1 quart

You'll find below a list of things that every good cook should know. But this is the most important tip: **work with an adult.** This is the safe way for you to work in the kitchen. Cooking together is fun, too. It's a tradition American families have always shared. Keep it alive today!

1. Choose a time that suits you and the adult who's cooking with you, so that you will both enjoy working together in the kitchen.

2. Wash your hands with soap before and after you handle food. Wear an apron, tie back your hair, and roll up your sleeves.

3. Read a recipe carefully, all the way through, before you start it. Look at the pictures. They will help you understand the steps.

4. Gather all the ingredients and equipment you will need before you start to cook. Put everything where you can reach it easily.

5. Ask an adult to show you how to peel, cut, and grate with sharp kitchen tools. Always use a chopping board to save kitchen counters.

6. Pay attention while using knives so that you don't cut your fingers! Remember—a good, sharp knife is safer than a dull one.

7. When you stir or mix, hold the bowl or pan steady on a flat surface, not in your arms.

8. Make sure your mixing bowls, pots, and pans are the right size. If they are too small, you'll probably spill. If pots and pans are too large, foods will burn more easily.

9. Clean up spills right away.

10. Pots and pans will be less likely to spill on the stove if you turn the handles toward the side.

11. Have an adult handle hot pans. Don't use the stove burners or the oven without permission or supervision.

12. Turn off the burner or the oven as soon as a dish is cooked.

13. Potholders and oven mitts will protect you from burns. Use them when you touch anything hot. Protect kitchen counters by putting trivets or cooling racks under hot pots and pans.

14. Keep hot foods hot and cold foods cold. If you plan to make things early and serve them later, store them properly. Foods that could spoil belong in the refrigerator. Wrap foods well.

15. If you decide to make a whole meal, be sure to plan so that all the food will be ready when you are ready to serve it.

16. Cleanup is part of cooking, too. Leave the kitchen at least as clean as you found it. Wash all the dishes, pots, and pans. Sweep the floor. Throw away the garbage.

COOKBOOKS IN THE 1940S

It was hard for home-front cooks to plan balanced meals because many familiar foods were rationed. Cookbooks were filled with tips to make cooking and meal planning quick and easy. Many wartime cookbooks gave a month's worth of menus that didn't use rationed food at all.

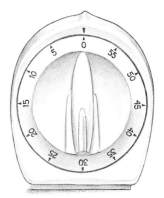

TIMING

When a recipe gives two cooking times— for example, when it says, "bake 25 to 30 minutes"—first set the timer for the shorter time. If the food is not done when the timer rings, give it more time.

BREAKFAST

Busy home-front families appreciated quick-to-fix breakfast foods.

Soldiers fighting far away needed every bit of food that America could send them. So families on the home front were extra careful not to waste food. They knew that wasting food meant wasting something that America needed to win the war.

Home-front families quickly learned that food wasn't the only thing that could be wasted. Time became precious, too, because many women had to rush off each morning to wartime jobs. While Molly and her brothers and sister rushed to get ready for school, Mom rushed right along with them to get ready for work. Now that Mom was working at the Red Cross, she needed help with cooking and cleaning.

Mrs. Gilford rose to the challenge. She arrived on the dot of seven o'clock every weekday morning to cook and clean for Molly and her family. She wasted no time getting straight to work making breakfast. Soon the kitchen was warm and steamy and the sweet, cinnamony smell of Mrs. Gilford's quick coffee cake filled the house. She also fortified the McIntire family with grapefruit halves and orange juice, both rich in "victory vitamin C."

Molly looked forward to weekend mornings. Everybody was more relaxed, and there was more time to make a bigger breakfast. On Friday nights, Molly mixed up a batch of her famous fruit cups and put them into the freezer for a special weekend breakfast treat. In Molly's time, freezers were very small. They had room for a few trays of ice cubes and little else!

On Saturday mornings, Molly and Mom liked to cook breakfast while they were still in their pajamas. While Mom fried bacon and potatoes, Molly made toad-in-a-hole. Mom helped Molly drop an egg into the hole in each slice of bread. It took practice to get her aim just right!

BREAKFAST

★

Fried Potatoes

•

Toad-in-a-Hole

•

Fried Bacon

•

Quick Coffee Cake

•

Frozen Fruit Cups

In the 1940s, milk was delivered to many homes each morning.

FRIED POTATOES

In 1944, some experts thought children should eat four potatoes every day to be healthy!

INGREDIENTS

4-6 potatoes, cooked
   and chilled
Bacon drippings or
   cooking oil to coat skillet
Salt and pepper

EQUIPMENT

Paper towels
Knife
Cutting board
Large skillet
Spatula

DIRECTIONS   *6 servings*

1. Place 3 layers of paper towels on the counter next to the stove.

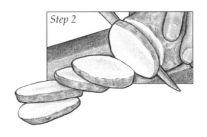
Step 2

2. Cut the cooked potatoes into thin slices. They will taste even better if the skins are left on!

3. Coat the bottom of the skillet with bacon drippings or oil. Heat the skillet over medium-high heat.

4. Cover the bottom of the skillet with potato slices. Sprinkle salt and pepper on them.

Step 5

5. When the bottoms of the slices are brown, use the spatula to turn them over to brown the other side.

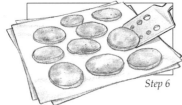
Step 6

6. Use the spatula to put the fried potatoes on the paper towels to drain.

7. Continue frying the rest of the potato slices in the same way. If the potatoes stick, add more bacon drippings or oil to the skillet. ★

TOAD-IN-A-HOLE

INGREDIENTS

6 slices of bread
Butter
6 eggs

EQUIPMENT

Drinking glass or
   cookie cutter
Butter knife
Large skillet
Measuring spoons
Spatula
Serving plate

Molly used her best aim to drop these eggs into their bread frames.

DIRECTIONS   *6 servings*

1. Use the drinking glass or cookie cutter to cut a hole in the center of each bread slice. Then butter 1 side of each slice.

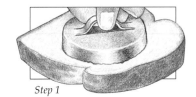
Step 1

2. Heat the skillet over low heat. Add 1 tablespoon of butter, using the spatula to coat the skillet evenly as the butter melts.

3. Put 2 slices of bread into the skillet, buttered side down. Crack an egg into the hole in each slice. When the slices are golden brown on the bottom, turn them over with the spatula.

Step 3

4. When the bread is browned on the bottom and the eggs are cooked, use the spatula to move each toad-in-a-hole onto the serving plate. Cook the remaining bread and eggs the same way. ★

EGGS

Eggs were not rationed during the war. In September 1944, eggs cost 51 cents a dozen, or about 4 cents each. How much does an egg cost today?

9

FRIED BACON

*Molly saved bacon drippings
to use in other recipes.*

INGREDIENTS

12 slices of lean bacon

EQUIPMENT

Paper towels
Large skillet
Fork or tongs
Metal can to store
  bacon drippings
Ovenproof plate

DIRECTIONS   *6 servings*

1. Place 3 layers of paper towels on the counter next to the stove.

2. Carefully separate 6 bacon slices and place them side by side in the skillet. Turn the heat to medium high.

3. Have an adult help you cook the slices until the edges start to curl. Stand back a little from the skillet while the bacon cooks. Sometimes the grease splatters.

Step 4

4. Use the fork or tongs to turn each slice to cook the other side.

5. Continue cooking until the white fat begins to turn golden brown.

6. Turn each slice again and cook for another minute, or until the bacon is as crispy as you like it.

SAVE THAT FAT!

Families sometimes took cans of cooking fat to the butcher's shop. The fat could be exchanged for red points to buy meat. Glycerin (GLIS-er-in) from the fat was used to make gunpowder. One pound of cooking fat had enough glycerin to make more than a pound of gunpowder.

7. Turn off the heat. Use the fork or tongs to move each slice from the skillet to the paper towels to drain.

8. Have an adult pour the hot bacon drippings into a metal can. You can use the drippings in other recipes.

9. Fry the other 6 slices of bacon the same way.

10. Put the bacon on the plate and keep it warm in a 200° oven until you are ready to eat. ★

These children are turning in their weekly collections of fat and grease.

QUICK COFFEE CAKE

Fresh-baked coffee cake was a quick way to start a busy day in 1944.

INGREDIENTS

Shortening to grease pan
1 1/2 cups flour
2 teaspoons baking powder
1/2 teaspoon salt
3 tablespoons shortening
1/3 cup sugar
1 egg
2/3 cup milk
1 tablespoon butter
1/2 cup brown sugar
1 teaspoon cinnamon

EQUIPMENT

Paper towels
8-inch square baking pan
Sifter
Medium mixing bowl
Measuring cups and spoons
Large mixing bowl
Electric mixer
Rubber spatula
Wooden spoon
Small saucepan
Small bowl
Potholders
Knife

DIRECTIONS   *6 servings*

Step 2

Step 4

1. Preheat the oven to 425°. Use paper towels to grease the baking pan with shortening.

2. Put the sifter into the medium mixing bowl. Measure the flour, baking powder, and salt into the sifter and sift them into the bowl.

3. Measure 3 tablespoons of shortening into the large mixing bowl. Have an adult help you use the electric mixer to beat the shortening until it is creamy.

4. Slowly add the sugar to the shortening and beat until fluffy. Turn off the mixer. Scrape the sides of the bowl with the rubber spatula.

5. Crack the egg into the large mixing bowl. Add the milk. Beat well with the electric mixer, and then turn off the mixer. Scrape the sides of the bowl with the rubber spatula.

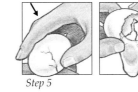
Step 5

6. Add the dry ingredients to the large mixing bowl. Stir them with the wooden spoon just enough to get them completely wet. Pour the mixture into the greased baking pan.

7. Melt the butter in the saucepan over low heat.

8. Mix the brown sugar and cinnamon in a small bowl. Stir in the melted butter.

9. Sprinkle this mixture over the batter in the baking pan.

10. Bake the coffee cake for 25 minutes or until golden brown.

11. Have an adult remove the coffee cake from the oven. Let it cool for a few minutes, cut it into pieces, and serve. ★

IS THAT REALLY BUTTER?

When butter was in short supply, home-front cooks used margarine. People mixed margarine, which was white, with yellow dye from a pellet to make it look more like butter. One company sold a plastic bag of margarine with the pellet already in it. Children tossed the bag back and forth to break the pellet!

FROZEN FRUIT CUPS

This frozen fruit treat is perfect for breakfast or anytime!

INGREDIENTS

1 cup fresh orange juice
15-ounce can of crushed
  pineapple, in its own
  juice
7-ounce can of mandarin
  oranges
1 pint strawberries
2 bananas
1½ cups ginger ale

EQUIPMENT

Measuring cup with spout
Large mixing bowl
Can opener
Knife
Cutting board
Mixing spoon
5-ounce paper
  drinking cups
Wax paper or
  plastic wrap

DIRECTIONS   *12 small cups*

1. Measure the orange juice into the mixing bowl.

2. Open the cans of crushed pineapple and mandarin oranges.

3. Add the pineapple and its juice to the mixing bowl.

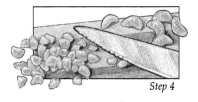

Step 4

4. Drain the juice from the mandarin oranges into the sink. Then cut the mandarin oranges into small pieces and add them to the mixing bowl.

Step 5

5. Wash the strawberries. Use the knife to remove the stems and cut the strawberries into small pieces. Add the strawberries to the mixing bowl.

6. Peel the bananas and cut them into small pieces. Add the bananas to the mixing bowl.

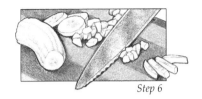

Step 6

7. Stir the fruits and juices together, and then stir in the ginger ale.

8. Use the measuring cup to pour the fruit mixture into small paper cups.

9. Cover the top of each cup loosely with wax paper or plastic wrap.

10. Put the cups into the freezer for several hours or overnight. ★

MISS CHIQUITA

The United Fruit Company introduced Miss Chiquita to sell its bananas in 1944. By 1947, stickers with her picture were placed on every bunch of Chiquita bananas sold in America. You can still see her picture on bananas today!

This picture shows Carmen Miranda, an actress who became famous in the 1940s for wearing fake fruit on her head!

DINNER

I n Molly's time, foods were divided into the Basic Seven Food Groups on a chart that government experts made to help home-front Americans plan good healthy meals. Americans wanted an easy way to know how much of each group to eat. Experts told them to divide each dollar they spent on food this way:

30¢ or more for Groups One, Two, and Three
20¢ or more for Group Four
25¢ or less for Group Five
15¢ or less for Group Six
10¢ or less for Group Seven

Molly's dinner included foods from every one of the Basic Seven Food Groups. Vitamin A salad had foods from four different groups. Crunchy carrots came from Group One. Crisp, leafy lettuce was from Group Two. Group Three fruits—lemons and apricots—added even more vitamins and minerals. And creamy cottage cheese, which is full of vitamin D, was from Group Four.

Milk and dairy products from Group Four were especially important for children, who were supposed to drink at least four glasses of milk a day. So Molly made her volcano potatoes with milk and put cheddar cheese on top of them.

A 1940s kitchen cupboard.

Vitality meat loaf had three powerful foods from Group Five—beef, pork, and eggs—along with both wheat germ and oatmeal from Group Six. Butter, margarine, and oil from Group Seven were rationed during World War Two. So Molly used only a little mayonnaise, which is made with oil, when she made deviled eggs for dinner.

Today, we try to eat less butter, sugar, and meat, just as Molly did. Molly ate less of those foods because they were rationed. We eat less of them today because we know we'll be healthier!

DINNER

Vitamin A Salad

•

Deviled Eggs

•

Carrot Curls and Celery Fans

•

Vitality Meat Loaf

•

Parsley Biscuits

•

Volcano Potatoes

•

Applesauce Cupcakes

VITAMIN A SALAD

This vitamin-packed salad is made with Jell-O®, a popular salad ingredient in Molly's time.

INGREDIENTS

3-ounce package of lemon
   gelatin
1 cup hot water
1 lemon
1 cup apricot nectar
1 cup cottage cheese
2 large carrots
15-ounce can of apricots,
   in their own juice
Lettuce leaves

EQUIPMENT

Mixing bowl
Measuring cups
   and spoons
Mixing spoon
Knife
Cutting board
Gelatin mold or aluminum
   bowl to use as a mold
Vegetable peeler
Grater
Can opener
Plastic wrap
Serving platter

DIRECTIONS   *6 servings*

1. Put the gelatin into the mixing bowl. Have an adult pour the hot water over the gelatin and stir until the gelatin is dissolved.

Step 2

2. Cut the lemon in half. Then squeeze one half of the lemon over the tablespoon until it is filled. Add the juice to the gelatin and water.

3. Add the apricot nectar to the gelatin mixture. Stir well.

4. Rinse the gelatin mold or aluminum bowl in cold water.

Because sugar was in short supply, home-front cooks used honey, fruits, and fruit juices to sweeten foods.

5. Pour 1 cup of gelatin into the bottom of the mold. Spoon the cottage cheese into the gelatin.

6. Pour another ½ cup of gelatin over the cottage cheese and gelatin mixture.

7. Place the bowl in the refrigerator while you prepare the rest of the salad.

8. Peel the carrots, making sure to peel away from yourself.

Step 8

9. Then grate the carrots and measure 1 cup of grated carrots.

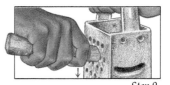

Step 9

10. Open the can of apricots. Drain the liquid into the sink. Then cut the apricots into small cubes.

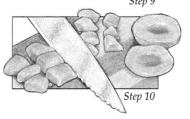

Step 10

11. Add the carrots and apricots to the remaining gelatin. Stir well.

12. Take the molded gelatin out of the refrigerator. It should be partially thickened. Spoon the carrot-apricot-gelatin mixture on top.

13. Cover the mold or bowl with plastic wrap and refrigerate it for several hours or overnight, until the gelatin is firmly set.

14. Cover the serving platter with fresh lettuce leaves. Then take the gelatin mold out of the refrigerator. Dip the mold or bowl into warm water at the sink, and then turn it over onto the serving platter. ★

JELL-O®

Jell-O was first sold in 1897. It was popular during World War Two when ads told "double-duty" housewives, who worked at home and at wartime jobs, how quick and easy it was to make.

DEVILED EGGS

Pretty foods add zest to meals—and eggs are packed with protein, too.

INGREDIENTS

6 hard-boiled eggs, peeled
3 tablespoons mayonnaise
1 teaspoon prepared
  mustard
1/4 teaspoon salt
1/4 teaspoon pepper
1 tablespoon pickle
  relish *(optional)*
Paprika

EQUIPMENT

Knife
Cutting board
2 spoons
Small mixing bowl
Plate
Fork
Measuring spoons

DIRECTIONS   *6 servings*

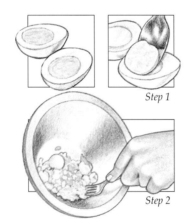

Step 1

1. Slice the eggs in half lengthwise. Scoop out the egg yolks and put them into the mixing bowl. Put the egg whites onto the plate.

2. Mash the yolks with the fork. Stir in the mayonnaise, mustard, salt, and pepper. Mix until smooth. Stir in a tablespoon of pickle relish if you like.

Step 2

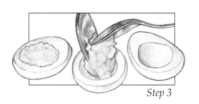

Step 3

3. Use 2 spoons to put the yolk mixture back into the whites. Try to fill each of the 12 halves equally. Sprinkle each deviled egg with a little paprika before serving. ★

HOW TO
HARD-BOIL EGGS

Put the eggs into a pan and cover them with water. Heat the water until it bubbles rapidly. Then turn off the heat and cover the pan. After 15 minutes, have an adult run cold water over the eggs. Then peel them.

*Fred MacMurray and Claudette Colbert starred in the 1947 movie, **The Egg and I.***

CARROT CURLS AND CELERY FANS

INGREDIENTS

3 large, crisp carrots
3 ribs of crisp celery

EQUIPMENT

Knife
Cutting board
Vegetable peeler
Toothpicks
Large bowl of ice water

Fancy vegetable frills like these look tricky, but they're easy to make.

DIRECTIONS   *6 servings*

1. Cut off the top and end from each carrot.

2. Peel the carrots, and then use the peeler to make long, wide carrot slices.

3. Curl each carrot strip around your finger. Have an adult help you stick a toothpick through each curl to hold it together.

Step 2

Step 3

4. Soak the carrot curls in ice water for 1 hour to help the carrots keep their curl. Remove the toothpicks before serving.

5. Rinse the celery with cold water. Cut off the top and end of each rib.

6. Cut each rib into 3 pieces of equal length. Cut the pieces in half lengthwise to make sticks.

7. Cut 3 or 4 slits into each celery stick as shown. Soak the celery in ice water for 1 hour, or until the fans curl. ★

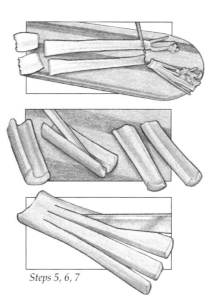

Steps 5, 6, 7

VITALITY MEAT LOAF

*The protein in this meat loaf gave
Molly vim, vigor, and vitality!*

INGREDIENTS

1 medium onion
1/4 cup fresh parsley
1 pound ground beef
1/2 pound ground pork
1/2 cup wheat germ
1 cup oatmeal
1 egg
1 cup evaporated milk
2 teaspoons salt
1/2 teaspoon pepper
1 teaspoon sage
1/2 teaspoon celery salt
1/4 cup chili sauce

EQUIPMENT

Knife
Cutting board
Large mixing bowl
Mixing spoon
Measuring cups
  and spoons
Loaf pan
Baking dish, 9 by 13 inches
Potholders

DIRECTIONS   *8 servings*

1. Preheat the oven to 350°.

2. Have an adult chop the onion into small pieces.

3. Wash and dry the parsley. Chop it into small pieces.

Step 3

4. Add the ground beef, ground pork, onion, and parsley to the mixing bowl.

5. Use the spoon to mix them together. Or wash your hands and mix the ingredients together with your fingers!

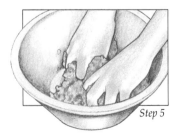
Step 5

6. Then add the rest of the ingredients. Mix them together the same way.

7. Pack the mixture firmly into the loaf pan.

8. Then turn the loaf pan over onto the baking dish so the meat loaf comes out.

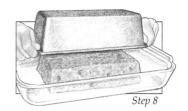

Step 8

9. Bake the meat loaf for 1 hour.

10. Have an adult remove the meat loaf from the oven. Let it cool for a few minutes, and then cut it into slices and serve. ★

SOLDIERS IN SPAMVILLE

Spam®, canned meat that tastes like ham, was part of almost every soldier's diet because it was nutritious and easy to fix. Soldiers ate it fried, baked, breaded, and even creamed. Soon they got tired of eating it and started making fun of it, like the soldiers who built "Spamville," shown in this picture.

PARSLEY BISCUITS

Fresh parsley from the Victory garden dresses up these simple biscuits.

INGREDIENTS

2 cups flour
2 teaspoons baking
 powder
$\frac{1}{2}$ teaspoon salt
1 teaspoon sugar
4 tablespoons shortening
$\frac{1}{2}$ cup fresh parsley
$\frac{3}{4}$ cup milk
Extra flour to coat
 your hands

EQUIPMENT

Sifter
Medium mixing bowl
Measuring cups
 and spoons
Fork or pastry cutter
Knife
Cutting board
Wooden spoon
Round cookie cutter
Cookie sheet
Potholders
Basket
Cloth napkin
Spatula

DIRECTIONS   *12 biscuits*

1. Preheat the oven to 425°.

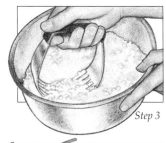
Step 2

2. Put the sifter into the mixing bowl. Measure the flour, baking powder, salt, and sugar into the sifter. Sift the dry ingredients into the mixing bowl.

Step 3

3. Measure the shortening into the mixing bowl. Use the fork or pastry cutter to blend the shortening into the dry ingredients until the mixture forms a crumbly dough.

Step 4

4. Wash and dry the parsley. Cut it into small pieces.

5. Use the wooden spoon to mix the milk and parsley into the dough.

6. Wash your hands and dry them. Put a little flour on your hands. Then put the dough on the cutting board. Pat the dough out until it is about ¹/2 inch thick.

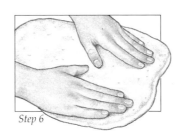
Step 6

7. Use the cookie cutter to cut out biscuits. Place the biscuits onto the cookie sheet.

Step 7

8. Bake the biscuits for 15 minutes or until they are golden brown.

9. Have an adult remove the parsley biscuits from the oven. Let them cool for a few minutes.

10. Line a pretty basket with a cloth napkin. Then use the spatula to move the biscuits into the serving basket. ★

CONVENIENCE FOODS

Prepackaged mixes made life easier for double-duty housewives in the 1940s. During the war, biscuit, muffin, pudding, and cake mixes were available in stores. By the end of the 1940s, cooks could buy mixes for rolls, cornbread, and pancakes, too.

VOLCANO POTATOES

These creamy potatoes erupt with cheddar cheese!

INGREDIENTS

6 large potatoes
2 tablespoons butter
1 teaspoon salt
¼ teaspoon pepper
½ cup milk
2 egg yolks
Shortening to grease
    baking dish
6 tablespoons grated
    cheddar cheese
Dash of paprika

EQUIPMENT

Vegetable peeler
Knife
Cutting board
2-quart saucepan with lid
Fork
Colander
Electric mixer
Measuring cup
    and spoons
Paper towels
Baking dish, 9 by 13 inches
Wooden spoon
Rubber spatula
Potholders
Metal spatula
Dinner plates

DIRECTIONS   *6 servings*

Step 1

1. Have an adult help you peel the potatoes, and then cut each potato into 4 pieces.

2. Put the potatoes into the saucepan. Add enough cold water to cover them.

3. Turn the heat on high and bring the water to a *boil*. Large bubbles will burst on the surface when the water boils.

4. Turn down the heat until the water *simmers*, or bubbles slightly. Put the lid on the saucepan and cook the potatoes for 20 minutes.

Families learned to grow their own potatoes in backyard Victory gardens.

5. After 20 minutes, insert the fork into a potato piece. If it goes in easily, the potatoes are done.

6. Place the colander in the sink. Have an adult take the hot pan of potatoes to the sink to pour the water through the colander.

7. Put the potatoes back into the saucepan. Use the electric mixer to beat the potatoes until they are smooth.

8. Add the butter, salt, pepper, milk, and egg yolks. Have an adult help you beat the potatoes with the electric mixer until they are light and fluffy.

9. Preheat the oven to 350°. Use paper towels to grease the baking dish with shortening. Spoon 6 mounds of mashed potatoes, each about 3 inches high, into the baking dish.

10. Use the rubber spatula to shape the potatoes into volcanoes. Use the spoon to make a crater in the top of each volcano.

11. Fill each volcano with a tablespoon of grated cheese. Sprinkle paprika on top.

12. Bake the volcano potatoes until the cheese melts and browns slightly.

13. Have an adult remove the potatoes from the oven. Use a metal spatula to loosen the potatoes carefully from the bottom of the baking dish. Lift them directly onto each dinner plate. ★

HOW TO SEPARATE EGGS

1. Crack the eggshell by tapping it lightly on the edge of a bowl.

2. Use your thumbs to divide the eggshell into 2 pieces, catching the egg yolk in 1 piece.

3. Carefully move the egg yolk to the other piece of eggshell, letting the egg white drop into the sink or a bowl.

Step 10

Step 13

27

APPLESAUCE CUPCAKES

Molly could make these delicious cupcakes even when sugar and butter were in short supply.

INGREDIENTS

2 cups flour, sifted
1 teaspoon baking soda
$\frac{1}{2}$ teaspoon ground nutmeg
$\frac{1}{2}$ teaspoon ground cinnamon
$\frac{1}{4}$ teaspoon ground cloves
$\frac{1}{4}$ teaspoon salt
$\frac{1}{3}$ cup shortening
$\frac{3}{4}$ cup honey
1 cup unsweetened applesauce
1 cup seedless raisins
$\frac{1}{4}$ cup broken walnut pieces
Your favorite frosting

EQUIPMENT

Cupcake or muffin pans
16 paper cupcake liners
Sifter
Medium mixing bowl
Measuring cups and spoons
Large mixing bowl
Electric mixer
Rubber spatula
Wooden spoon
Potholders
Toothpick
Wire cooling racks
Butter knife

DIRECTIONS   *16 cupcakes*

1. Preheat the oven to 350°. Line the cupcake pans with paper liners.

Step 2

2. Put the sifter into the medium mixing bowl. Measure the sifted flour, baking soda, nutmeg, cinnamon, cloves, and salt into the sifter. Sift these dry ingredients into the bowl.

3. Measure the shortening into the large mixing bowl. Have an adult help you use the electric mixer to beat the shortening until it is fluffy.

4. Add the honey to the shortening and continue to beat the mixture for 2 minutes. Stop the mixer once or twice and use the rubber spatula to scrape down the sides of the bowl.

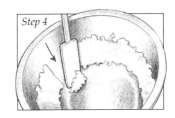
Step 4

5. Add half the applesauce and half the sifted dry ingredients to the honey and shortening mixture. Mix at medium speed until all the flour disappears. Stop once or twice to scrape down the sides of the bowl with the spatula.

6. Add the remaining applesauce and dry ingredients. Mix again until everything is blended.

Some farmers did not go to war. They were needed on the home front to grow fresh fruits and vegetables.

7. Use the wooden spoon to stir in the raisins and walnut pieces.

8. Spoon the batter into the cupcake liners, filling each about 2/3 full.

Step 8

9. Bake the cupcakes for 25 to 30 minutes.

10. Have an adult help you poke a toothpick into the center of a cupcake. If the toothpick comes out clean, the cupcakes are done. Set them on the racks to cool.

11. After 10 minutes, take the cupcakes out of the pans and let them cool completely on the racks before frosting them. ★

FAVORITE FOODS

Molly, Linda, and Susan walked home together each day after school. On days when they stopped at Molly's house to play, Molly made her two after-school specialties— PBJ roll-ups and jelly flags. She made them with bread that Mrs. Gilford baked each week.

Making bread was one of the things Mrs. Gilford did to help the war effort. Molly loved to help sift the flour—she could make a mess and not get into trouble! Nut-and-raisin bread was one of Molly's favorites. It was baked in an old coffee can. Once Mrs. Gilford tried to enrich her white bread by adding tomato juice to the dough. Her "pepped-up" bread had extra vitamins, but it was pink! Molly begged her not to make it again.

"Food is the mightiest weapon of them all," pamphlets and posters said to Americans who were hoping and working for victory. "FOOD FIGHTS FOR FREEDOM." For patriotic Americans, eating healthy food was a surefire way to help win World War Two. It gave them the energy they needed to do their part for the war effort. Molly helped grow vegetables in the family's backyard Victory garden. That way, there would be more canned vegetables to send to soldiers. Molly and Mom used fresh vegetables to make foods like vitamin-packed Victory garden soup, and they "canned" the rest in glass jars.

Americans said "V is for Victory" during World War Two. *V* was also for *Vigor* and *Vim*, the pep that helped everyone on the home front do important wartime work. Home-front cooks understood

"We'll have lots to eat this winter, won't we Mother?"

Grow your own
Can your own

that pep came from another big V—vitamins. When Molly was a girl, more Americans than ever knew that good food and vitamins build healthy bodies.

FAVORITE FOODS

French Toast

•

Waldorf Salad

•

PBJ Roll-Ups

•

Jelly Flags

•

Victory Garden Soup

•

Nut-and-Raisin Bread

•

Fruit Bars

FRENCH TOAST

Molly made French toast with old bread—a practical way to prevent waste!

INGREDIENTS

2 eggs
$\frac{1}{4}$ teaspoon salt
$\frac{2}{3}$ cup milk
1 tablespoon butter
6 slices of bread
Your favorite syrup

EQUIPMENT

Medium mixing bowl
Fork
Skillet
Spatula
Serving platter

DIRECTIONS   *6 servings*

Step 1

1. Crack the eggs into the mixing bowl and beat them with the fork. Mix in the salt and milk to make a batter.

2. Melt the butter in the skillet over medium-high heat and use the spatula to spread it evenly on the bottom.

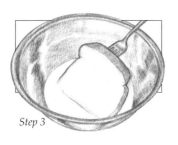

Step 3

3. Dip a bread slice into the egg batter. Have an adult help you put the slice into the hot skillet.

4. Dip another slice of bread into the egg batter and add it to the skillet.

Step 5

5. Cook the bread until the bottoms are golden brown. Then use the spatula to turn each slice of bread over and brown it on the other side.

6. Use the spatula to move the French toast from the skillet to the platter. Then cook the rest of the bread the same way. Serve the French toast with your favorite syrup! ★

WALDORF SALAD

INGREDIENTS

4 apples
2 tablespoons lemon juice
3 celery ribs
1/2 cup mayonnaise
Lettuce leaves
1/3 cup chopped walnuts

EQUIPMENT

Apple corer
Knife
Cutting board
Measuring cups
  and spoons
Mixing bowl
Mixing spoon
Serving plate

This salad was invented by a chef at the Waldorf-Astoria Hotel in New York City.

DIRECTIONS   *6 servings*

1. Insert the apple corer into the center of each apple and twist it to cut around the core. Remove the cores from the apples.

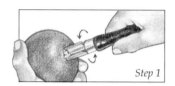
Step 1

2. Cut the apples into small cubes. Measure 2 cups of diced apples into the mixing bowl and sprinkle the lemon juice over them.

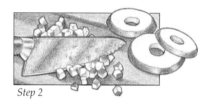
Step 2

3. Cut the tops and bottoms off the celery ribs. Then cut each rib into small cubes. Measure 1 cup of diced celery.

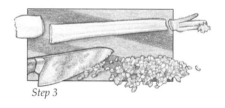
Step 3

4. Add the celery and mayonnaise to the apples, stirring well.

5. Cover the serving plate with fresh lettuce leaves. Pile the Waldorf salad on top of the lettuce, and then sprinkle it with chopped walnuts. ★

FRUIT DELIVERY

Fruit was not rationed during World War Two, but sometimes it was hard to get. Trucks that delivered fruit to grocery stores sometimes couldn't travel as far or as often as they could before the war because gasoline was rationed.

PBJ ROLL-UPS

Roll an old favorite into a new shape!

INGREDIENTS

Thin-sliced bread
Your favorite peanut
  butter
Your favorite jelly

EQUIPMENT

Butter knife
Sharp knife
Cutting board
Toothpicks
Wax paper

DIRECTIONS

1. For each serving, use 2 pieces of bread. Spread each piece with peanut butter. Then top the peanut butter with jelly.

2. Trim off the crusts on the cutting board. Save the crusts to feed to the birds.

Step 2

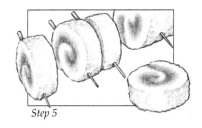
Step 3

3. Have an adult help you roll each slice of bread, spread side in. Fasten each roll with 4 toothpicks.

4. Wrap the rolls in wax paper and chill them in the refrigerator for 2 hours.

5. When you're ready to eat, remove the wax paper and cut each roll into slices. Then remove the toothpicks and serve the sandwiches. ★

Step 5

PEANUT-BUTTER PROTEIN

*In the 1940s, protein from meat was called **first-class** protein. **Second-class** protein came from plants like peanuts. Some people thought only first-class protein could make them strong. Today we know that protein from all sources is equally good for our bodies.*

Peanut-butter sandwiches are a good source of second-class protein.

JELLY FLAGS

These patriotic snacks are so delicious, they deserve a salute!

INGREDIENTS

Thin-sliced bread
Soft butter
Your favorite red jelly
  or jam

EQUIPMENT

Butter knife
Sharp knife
Cutting board
Wax paper

DIRECTIONS

1. For 2 servings, use 3 slices of bread. Spread a thin layer of butter onto each slice. Cover the butter with jelly or jam. Spread it thickly all the way to the edges.

2. Stack the slices on top of each other. Top the stack with a piece of plain bread. Use the sharp knife to trim off the crusts on the cutting board. Save the crusts to feed to the birds.

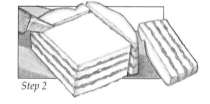

Step 2

3. Wrap the sandwiches in wax paper. Chill them in the refrigerator for 2 hours.

4. When you're ready to eat, unwrap the jelly bread and slice it into 4 strips. Turn the strips on their sides to make striped flags. ★

Step 4

1944 SHOPPING LIST

	Cost	Points
1 pound butter	46¢	16
1 pound grape jam	21¢	0
1 loaf bread	10¢	0

35

VICTORY GARDEN SOUP

This thick soup with chunks of garden vegetables was so good that Molly didn't even mind the turnips!

INGREDIENTS

1 medium potato
1 small onion
1 rib of celery
1 large carrot
1 medium turnip
$\frac{1}{2}$ cup corn
$\frac{1}{2}$ cup peas
1 tomato
3 lettuce leaves
2 tablespoons butter
2 tablespoons flour
2 cups tomato juice
1 cup water
$\frac{1}{2}$ tablespoon salt
$\frac{1}{8}$ teaspoon pepper
$\frac{1}{4}$ cup alphabet macaroni

EQUIPMENT

Vegetable peeler
Knife
Cutting board
Medium saucepan
Measuring cups
  and spoons
Fork
Potato masher
Large soup pot
Wooden spoon

DIRECTIONS   *6 servings*

1. Have an adult help you peel the potato and then cut it into small cubes.

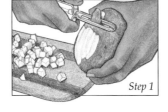
Step 1

2. Put the potato pieces into the saucepan and add just enough cold water to cover them.

VICTORY WITH VEGETABLES

A vegetable correctly cooked
Has color, health, and taste!
A vegetable that's murdered
In the pot is so much waste.
Use just a little water
And not too long a time—
Make your vegetables a perfect dish
And not a perfect crime!

— ***Coupon Cookery***, *a cookbook from Molly's time*

3. Put the saucepan onto the stove and turn the burner to medium high. When the water begins to *boil*, or bubble rapidly, turn the heat down. Let the potatoes *simmer*, or bubble gently, for 15 minutes.

4. While the potatoes simmer, have an adult help you prepare all the vegetables, as shown on the next page.

PREPARING VEGETABLES FOR SOUP

5. After 15 minutes, insert the fork into a potato piece. If it goes in easily, the potatoes are done.

6. Let the potatoes cool for a few minutes. Then mash them with the cooking water.

7. Put the butter into the soup pot and melt it over medium heat. Stir in the onions and celery. Cook them over low heat for about 5 minutes, stirring often.

8. Add the flour to the butter, onions, and celery in the soup pot. Stir for 1 minute over low heat.

9. Stir in the tomato juice, water, salt, pepper, and macaroni.

10. Turn up the heat to medium high. Add the potatoes, carrots, turnips, corn, peas, and tomato.

11. Cook the soup over medium-high heat, stirring occasionally. When it begins to boil, lower the heat and add the lettuce. Let the soup simmer for 20 minutes. ★

Chop the onion and celery into small pieces.

Peel the carrot. Slice it $\frac{1}{4}$ inch thick.

A store-bought turnip may be waxed. Cut off the wax with a vegetable peeler. Then dice the turnip into small cubes.

Slice fresh corn from the cob—or use frozen corn.

Remove fresh peas from the pod—or use frozen peas.

Cut the tomato into small chunks. Tear the lettuce leaves into 1-inch squares.

WASTE NOT, WANT NOT

Clever home-front cooks often added leftover vegetables to their hearty soups. Add your favorites to this soup. A little more of one vegetable or a little less of another won't hurt.

NUT-AND-RAISIN BREAD

Molly made this sweet bread in an old coffee can.

INGREDIENTS

3/4 cup white flour
3 teaspoons baking powder
1/4 teaspoon baking soda
1 teaspoon salt
3 tablespoons sugar
1 1/2 cups whole-wheat flour
1/3 cup chopped nuts
1/3 cup raisins
1 egg
1 tablespoon butter
1 1/4 cups milk
1/4 cup molasses
Shortening to grease can

EQUIPMENT

Sifter
Medium mixing bowl
Measuring cups and spoons
Mixing spoon
Large mixing bowl
Fork
Small saucepan
Electric mixer
Paper towels
Clean, empty 1-pound coffee can or 46-ounce juice can
Potholders
Wire cooling rack
Butter knife
Can opener

DIRECTIONS   *1 loaf*

1. Preheat the oven to 350°.

Step 2

2. Put the sifter into the medium mixing bowl. Measure the white flour, baking powder, baking soda, salt, and sugar into the sifter. Sift these dry ingredients into the bowl.

3. Measure the whole-wheat flour and mix it in with the other dry ingredients. Then add the chopped nuts and raisins to the flour mixture.

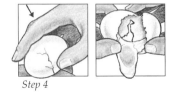

Step 4

4. Crack the egg into the large mixing bowl and beat it with the fork.

5. Melt the butter in the saucepan over low heat.

6. Add the melted butter, milk, and molasses to the egg in the large mixing bowl. Use the electric mixer to beat these ingredients together.

7. Add the dry ingredients to the large mixing bowl in small portions, mixing each portion well as it is added.

8. Use paper towels to grease the coffee can or juice can generously with shortening. Pour the batter into the can.

9. Bake for 1 hour. Then have an adult remove the bread from the oven and place it onto the rack to cool.

10. When the bread is cool, use the butter knife to loosen the bread from the sides of the can. Then use a can opener to open the bottom of the can and gently push out the loaf. ★

BREAD FOR SOLDIERS

Fresh-baked bread was important to soldiers. It kept their spirits up because it reminded them of home. The army thought fresh-baked bread was so important that bakery units were set up as close to the front lines as possible.

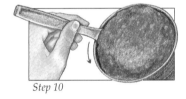

Step 10

THE GREATEST THING SINCE SLICED BREAD

In January 1943, government officials stopped the sale of sliced bread. They believed that sliced bread was often wasted because it went stale faster. Some people thought it was a silly idea and poked fun at the government's rule, as this picture shows!

FRUIT BARS

*These chewy bars are filled with fruit—
for lots of pep and get-up-and-go!*

INGREDIENTS

1 cup dried, pitted fruit,
   such as pears, dates,
   pineapples, or apricots
$\frac{1}{3}$ cup sugar
$\frac{1}{2}$ cup water
1 lemon
1 cup flour
1 cup brown sugar
$\frac{1}{2}$ teaspoon salt
8 tablespoons butter
$1\frac{1}{2}$ cups quick oatmeal
3 tablespoons milk
Shortening to grease pan

EQUIPMENT

Measuring cups
   and spoons
Knife
Cutting board
1-quart saucepan
Wooden spoon
Grater
Large mixing bowl
Fork or pastry cutter
Paper towels
Baking pan, 8 inches
   square
Potholders

DIRECTIONS   *24 small fruit bars*

1. Preheat the oven to 350°.

Step 2

2. Cut the dried fruit into small cubes. Put the diced fruit into the saucepan.

3. Add the sugar and water to the saucepan. Cook the fruit mixture over medium heat until it is thick, about 5 to 10 minutes, stirring often. Then turn down the heat to low.

4. Have an adult help you grate the *rind*, or outside, of the lemon. Measure 1 tablespoon of lemon rind and add it to the fruit mixture.

Step 4

Step 5

5. Cut the lemon in half. Squeeze one half of the lemon over a tablespoon until it is filled. Then stir the lemon juice into the fruit mixture.

6. Measure the flour, brown sugar, and salt into the mixing bowl.

7. Use the fork or pastry cutter to mix in the butter until the mixture is crumbly.

Step 7

8. Add the oatmeal and stir in the milk. Mix well.

9. Use paper towels to grease the baking pan with shortening.

10. Pack half of the oatmeal mixture into the bottom of the pan.

11. Spread the fruit mixture on top. Then spread the remaining oatmeal mixture over the fruit.

Step 11

12. Bake the fruit bars for 40 minutes.

13. Have an adult remove the pan from the oven. Let the pan cool completely. Then cut the fruit bars and serve. ★

DESSERTS FOR SOLDIERS

Ice cream was one of the best morale boosters soldiers could get. Some soldiers made their own version of ice cream in their airplanes. They put the ingredients into a large can and set the can in an unheated part of the plane. The vibrations from the plane mixed the ice cream while the cold temperature from being so high in the sky froze it!

PARTY IDEAS

SLUMBER PARTY FUN

At slumber parties in 1944, girls told secrets and stories, sneaked midnight snacks, and often tried to stay up all night. And their slumber parties usually included at least one pillow fight!

Parties during World War Two often were simpler than parties before the war because many foods were rationed and many people were busy with wartime jobs. Still, having fun was important. In fact, having fun was recognized as good for people's spirits during the war. Molly and her friends had lots of fun at slumber parties, just as you and your friends do today. Use some of these ideas to fill your next slumber party with 1940s fun!

★ **A BACKWARD SLUMBER PARTY**

Some children had backward parties in the 1940s. Write on your invitations that you are having a backward slumber party and that your guests should wear their clothes backward when they come. Greet each guest backward, by saying "good-bye" when they arrive and "hello" when they leave. Have a backward spelling bee, in which each guest tries to spell a simple word backward. Plan a backward race, where guests have to walk backward through an obstacle course. If you serve a meal, eat dessert first!

★ **AN INDOOR CAMP SLUMBER PARTY**

Cut stars from scraps of white paper (tinfoil was needed for the war!) and tape them to the ceiling. If your family has a small tent, ask permission to set it up indoors. If not, just sleep out under your paper stars! Ask your guests to come with flashlights to make a "flashlight campfire." You might want to sing campfire songs like "Home on the Range" or "Clementine." After the singing, tell scary stories around your flashlight campfire!

★ **A PATRIOTIC SLUMBER PARTY**

Ask your guests to wear red, white, and blue clothing to your party. Before the party, decorate a large sheet of poster board to look like an American flag, but without the stars. Then cut out 48 small stars from white paper. (In Molly's time, the flag only had 48 stars!) Attach tape to each star. When your guests arrive, play Pin the Star on the Flag. You can also play Musical Flags. Before the party, hide dozens of tiny flags around the room. Ask your guests to sit in a circle. Then begin playing patriotic music, like "The Star-Spangled Banner." When you stop the music, your guests gather as many flags as they can before you start the music again. The girl who has the most flags when you start the music again wins!

★ **A TOP-SECRET SLUMBER PARTY**

During World War Two, each country used codes to keep military messages secret from the enemy. Write invitations to your slumber party in your own secret code. Assign each letter of the alphabet a number. For example, the number *1* might stand for the letter *A*, *2* might stand for the letter *B*, and so on. Include a secret password that your guests must say at the door before they come in to your party. Be sure to put the key to the code on the back of the invitation so your guests will be able to understand your message! During your party, have a top-secret treasure hunt, with the clues written in code. Inexpensive rings make great hidden treasures. You and your friends can wear them as "secret agent" rings!

RAG CURLS

Girls in Molly's time loved to fix each other's hair at slumber parties. The girl in this picture has her hair set in rag curlers. To make them, wind a friend's hair around strips of fabric. Then tie the ends of each strip together. In the morning your friend will wake up with curly hair!

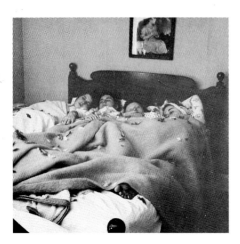

A PLACE TO SLUMBER

A slumber party can be too much "party" and not enough "slumber" for some of your guests. Some girls may want to try to stay up all night, while others want to get some shut-eye. If you can, set aside a room where guests can sleep without being disturbed.

Food

When you send your invitations, tell if your party will include snacks or a meal. Try making some of the recipes in this book. You can also make your own "ration stamps" with pictures of the foods and drinks you'll serve. Have your guests use stamps to "buy" what they'd like to eat and drink.

Place Settings

If your parents have Fiesta dishes, Depression glass, or other dinnerware from the 1940s, ask if you can use it for your party. Paper plates and cups were available in wartime, too, though people used them sparingly.

Decorations

Make simple homemade decorations for your party, just as Molly would have done. During the war, Americans couldn't get many store-bought decorations because factories were making war supplies instead.

Clothes

Girls could wear pants by the time Molly was a girl, and they also liked to wear white ankle socks and saddle shoes. Many girls wore men's-style pajamas in Molly's time, with tops and long pants.

Music

Girls like Molly liked to listen to music on the radio or to records on a phonograph. During the war, people liked to listen to patriotic songs like "You're a Grand Old Flag" and popular songs like "Chattanooga Choo-Choo." Your local library should have recordings of these songs.

AMERICAN GIRLS PASTIMES™
Activities from the Past for Girls of Today

You'll enjoy all the Pastimes books about your favorite characters in The American Girls Collection®.

Learn to cook foods that Felicity, Kirsten, Addy, Samantha, and Molly loved with the Pastimes **COOKBOOKS.** They're filled with great recipes and fun party ideas.

Make the same crafts that your favorite American Girls character made. Each of the **CRAFT BOOKS** has simple step-by-step instructions and fascinating historical facts.

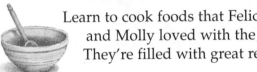

Imagine that you are your favorite American Girls character as you stage a play about her. Each of the **THEATER KITS** has four Play Scripts and a Director's Guide.

Learn about fashions of the past as you cut out the ten outfits in each of the **PAPER DOLL KITS.** Each kit also contains a make-it-yourself book plus historical fun facts.

There are **CRAFT KITS** for each character with directions and supplies to make 3 crafts from the Pastimes Craft Books. Craft Kits are available only through Pleasant Company's catalogue, which you can request by filling out the postcard below.

Turn the page to learn more about the other delights in The American Girls Collection. ⟶

I'm an American girl who loves to get mail. Please send me a catalogue of The American Girls Collection®:

My name is _____

My address is _____

City _____ State _____ Zip _____

Parent's signature _____

1961

And send a catalogue to my friend:

My friend's name is _____

Address _____

City _____ State _____ Zip _____

1225

THE AMERICAN GIRLS COLLECTION®

The American Girls Collection tells the stories of five lively nine-year-old girls who lived long ago—Felicity, Kirsten, Addy, Samantha, and Molly. You can read about their adventures in a series of beautifully illustrated books of historical fiction. By reading these books, you'll learn what growing up was like in times past.

There is also a lovable doll for each character with beautiful clothes and lots of wonderful accessories. The dolls and their accessories make the stories of the past come alive today for American girls like you.

The American Girls Collection is for you if you love to curl up with a good book. It's for you if you like to play with dolls and act out stories. It's for you if you want something so special that you will treasure it for years to come.

To learn more about The American Girls Collection, fill out the postcard on the other side of the page and mail it to Pleasant Company, or call **1-800-845-0005.** We will send you a free catalogue about all the books, dolls, dresses, and other delights in The American Girls Collection.